RANDOM THOUGHTS

Jennifer Johnson

Copyrights

Createspace.com 2018

Published via Kindle Direct Publishing

Summary of Contents:

Section One:

Random Thoughts

HOMELESS

It is remarkable that the amount of homeless people have almost doubled since the 1980's. An estimated 1% of the U.S. population experiences homelessness at some point every year. Since the 1980's the number of homeless people has been steadily increasing. The average number of homeless people during the 1980's rose from 200,000 individuals to almost 500,000. Almost 60% of these individuals lived in homeless shelters while the remaining 40% were unsheltered. The United States unlike many other countries around the world with higher homeless statistics has a beneficial characteristic that the condition of homelessness is temporary in almost 80% of the cases. Anywhere from 75% to 80% of people who fall homeless are able to find shelters, adequate affordable housing or any other permanent residence within 3 months of falling homeless, making homelessness a temporary rather than a permanent condition for the population in the United States. However, chronic homelessness affects an average of 20% to 25% of those individuals who fall homeless. Estimates represent that an average of 23% of homeless individuals are in the chronic condition of not finding adequate housing for more than 1 year from the moment in which they fall into homelessness. Statistics show that both young and elderly veterans are the demographic group more likely to fall into homelessness. Estimates cite that 40% of veterans who have survived and came back to the US are homeless, comprising a large portion of the male adult population who are homeless on a constant basis. Surveys conducted on recent homeless individuals represent that the main causes of their homelessness are lack of income, unemployment, poverty, and the inability to find affordable housing. An estimated 65% of those surveyed say that they are in homelessness due to one of these factors. However, surveys represent that other non-economic factors play a role in the situation of homelessness. Mental illness, substance abuse, drug addiction, alcohol addiction, parent abuse, disease, emotional distress, depression and other health problems. So why do these statistics bother me? How can this situation be helped? Granted there are shelters and programs available to help and often not everyone can be helped especially if they have placed themselves and continue to keep themselves in these circumstances. There are so many abandoned houses that could be utilized for housing and so many programs that could be used for job training. We could help teach these people to live on their own two feet again and give them a second chance. In my opinion; if they blow this second chance by drug use or criminal acts then they should be left to their own devices to fix their lives. We all know not everyone wants to fix or change where they stand. There are those out there who are placed in these predicaments who did not chose this lifestyle and struggle daily taking every opportunity they can to change and make life better. Often for the ones who do want to change and live better there aren't many resources for them to utilize to help them. My pet peeve is those who scam. The peddlers who have things managed and live decently but still go out and pretend to be homeless and need help. Those who give the ones who actually need help a bad name. You know who I am talking about. The beggar on the corner dressed in nice clothes with new Nike shoes smoking cigarettes holding up their sign that they are hungry. I'm sorry but if you can afford those cigarettes you can afford a dinner. If you can afford the Nike shoes you can go to a thrift shop and set yourself up a little better. There have been so many times I have seen these so called "homeless" walk to a nice car and switch out to another person. This is horrible scamming. These users are giving those who are trying and actually deserve the help a bad name. Then there are the ones; which is very mind boggling; who chose to be homeless. Who have admitted they have chosen to be traveling vagabonds free from "societies bonds". Those are the ones who need eliminated from help aid since they chose that lifestyle. I just can't imagine wanting to scourge for food and sleep in weird places but it seems to make them free and happy. I have seen in warmer climate areas where people have made permanent camp sites. That is their way of living and they are happy that way. To each their own I suppose. I just know there is a better way to take care of our fellow humans who deserve better lives. Everyone who wants a second chance and wants to work hard to prove themselves should have that opportunity. Unfortunately, life is not fair and often cruelest to the ones who don't deserve it the most.

WHAT MY DOG THINKS

I wish I knew what my dog is thinking sometimes. They obviously all have different personalities. I would especially love to peek into her mind when she is off staring into space. Is she daydreaming of chasing a cat? Is she pondering playing with a toy? I would love to know what she is thinking when she is staring at me at times with her big eyes focused and her ears up at attention. Is she silently mocking me and my baby talk to her? When she smiles is she happy with me? Is she begging for a treat? I wonder what runs through her mind as she naps on the couch wrapped up on my leg. I wonder what she is dreaming about as she whimpers and twitches in her sleep. Is she chasing an animal or destroying a toy? I wonder how she feels stretched out in the sun relaxing like I wish I could. Not a care in the world. I wonder what she thinks when she hears something outside.

Barking and carrying on. Is she trying to protect me or cure her own curiosity? Of course, there are several reasons I may not want to know. I love my pet because she doesn't mock me, make fun of me, or judge me. She doesn't argue or talk back. She doesn't care if I look crappy or if I am sassy. She always knows when I need a good cuddle and senses when I need her. She loves me no matter what. And If I knew what she was thinking I might not like her as much.

BLIND DREAMS

It is said that the blind can dream like those who can see. Some dreams are dependent on when they lost their sight. Some say they can still see pictures but believe it's what they imagine things would look like. They say they can see color although auditory is more prominent. I could not imagine losing my sight although I only have one eye now. I fear one day this is possible. I think that those who overcome this and live out life still happy in their own "sight" on things are amazing people. I value their ability to be missing something but still fill that void and remain happy in a different way. I believe it would be easier to handle if born blind rather than go blind. Adapting is easier when you are younger.

Challenges are not seen as so negative and life altering until you are older and feel the true changes it makes. I often wonder if they have curiosity of the way things really look knowing that descriptions of things can vary from person to person. Perhaps the imagination is the best way to go. Creating the world as the way you want to see it instead of the way it may really be. There are no judgments based on looks anymore. Everything would be based on what felt right. Helen Keller is one of my heroes. She not only overcame but became successful as well. She went beyond what people thought she could. She didn't let a disability stop her from being more.

MIND CONTROL

Imagine the possibility of possessing the ability to control another's thoughts. Perhaps reading another's thoughts. I don't think I would want anyone to know what was on my mind. This may cause people to develop such paranoias of the world or maybe techniques to block others out. I probably wouldn't want to know what others were thinking either. People are probably sicker and more twisted than I care to know. The only good I could see coming from this is to determine guilty or innocent in major crimes like murders. Other than that, I believe this ability would be more of a burden if not psychologically damaging. What if you have the ability to force your will upon another? I'm sure there have already been experiments conducted to do so. How unfair it would be for the victim of the controller? I can only imagine how this could increase kidnappings or crimes and the controller get away with saying it wasn't them and no evidence to prove otherwise. Granted this could be used for good. Perhaps to help another change their negative thought pattern into a positive one or use this power to cure the ill minded. Physiologists could use this ability to cure those with mental illnesses or phobias. But, alas, this is not our world. This power would most likely only be used for evil. For one to conduct their wills through another and get away with evil deeds; even murder.

THINGS CHANGE AFTER HIGH SCHOOL

I never thought about how much people change after high school and how much meaning stands from those years. I had my ten-year reunion and the people who never talked to me were like old friends. The people who picked on me and bullied me apologized and I forgave them. As kids we are all crazy. Now that I have a teenage daughter in high school I want her to know that the people she knows now will not be the same people later in life. I want her to know the trials and tribulations she faces now will have no meaning but a memory after high school. I had two best girlfriends who were there every step of the way and who mean the world to me even though we aren't as close or talk as much. It's also those years thy brought us together. Even to this day we know we still love each other and would be there. Even through life's chaos that made us miss weddings, holidays, and births there is still that bond. Even those people have changed. I want my daughters to know that friends like that are few and far between and to hold on to them. Even if it’s just in your heart.

WHAT WRITING MEANS TO ME

I had always dreamed of being published. I began writing poetry and journals when I was just 14. I had my first poem published in my school newspaper for prom about drinking and driving. I was told I had talent but I remained humble. I always wanted my life experiences to help others and to let know they are not alone in many of their life's journeys. We often all have similar trying experiences or heartbreaks. I always wanted my words to comfort others pain. I wanted to touch hearts. I wanted to relate, share, and maybe even change another's life path. When I began to publish my book, it was out of passion not profits. I didn't and still don't care if I make a single dime. Everyone should share their passions and what a better one to share than words? I want to inspire others and leave behind my own small legacy. It means the world to mean to see my children writing. I was beyond words when they published their own set of words for the world. It touches me to hear from readers who tell me when a poem or topic touched them or helped them. It touches my heart to hear them say thank you and tell me how they marked the page or read it more than once. That's what writing means to me; my passion touching another's heart!

SELF-PUBLISHING

The most challenging and rewarding way to publish yet. Design and write the material in any way you wish and bypass all the acceptance waiting from an agent or publishing company. Immediately express your words and self on paper and make it available through all the means of a normal author. The hard part.... Self-promotion. You have to have advertising and be able to sell yourself and your product like an entrepreneur. You must make yourself known and do readings and book signings. Then once you are known you must work at staying in your public's eye and being an upstanding person. All in all; it is all worth the hard work!!! Be proud of your work despite sales!! Be proud you accomplished what many are too scared or don't have the feeling of talent to do!!! Keep writing and publishing because you never know who you will inspire or touch!! That's what makes the work worth it!!!

BUCKET LIST

- Swim with the dolphins
- Travel to Nepal
- Publish a novel
- Travel to Egypt.
- Do an African safari.

- Watch my step daughters grow.
- Tell everyone how much I love them.
- Learn to play guitar.
- Learn to scuba dive.
- Publish lots of poetry.
- Meet Johnny Depp.
- Modeling.
- Donate to locks of love.
- Learn to cook better
- Learn to ride a horse
- Take my kids to Disney land
- take my husband to Alaska!
- Go somewhere haunted and see a ghost.
- Hike the Appalachian trail!
- Watch my kids graduate college.
- Go back to Australia
- Swim the Great Barrier Reef
- Fly in a Helicopter
- Go to Germany
- Explore a Castle in Ireland
- Inspire my children

What's on your list?

BLOGGING

I was told that to be successful blogger you must pick a subject and stick to it. I like to go against the grain I suppose. I like to blog about anything and everything that pops into my mind. Why limit yourself when the world is so big? Why not say and talk about things that others often wonder about but never speak of? I like to share my experiences and encourage others to do great things. I like to encourage others to express themselves and think outside the norm. Sometimes I like a good debate. I hope to relate and inspire someone. I hope my children learn from me. I like to do reviews or products and books or just share my struggles. It makes me find new ideas to research which means more learning and self-growth. Sometimes I just like talking about weird things!!

TIME FLIES

Isn't it amazing how the older get the faster time seems to pass us by? Before we know it, we are thinking of the good ole days and how big your kids have gotten. Is it because we are so busy that time just seems to go faster? I hear my children complain of boredom and I remember when I was a child that the days seemed to take forever. A week was an eternity. It seems as though there isn't enough time in a day for quality time and completing the things we need to get done. Christmas ends and before you know it you are buying gifts again. Seasons change faster every year and I feel like I didn't get to enjoy them. I put out decorations for holidays and change them again so quickly I wonder why I still put them out. In a full day of work, chores, and raising kid's bedtime comes too soon and I haven't done all that I have wanted to.

JAMAICA

Such a beautiful country. I loved visiting this island. The culture is so wonderful. The views no matter where you are on the island are majestic. I loved how our cab driver stuck by our side everywhere we went. My favorite part was climbing Dunn river falls! Climbing that waterfall was such a serene adventure!!!! The shopping was not for me. The people at the booths were a little too grabby for my attention. I'm a browser more than a buyer so it didn't set with me. I love learning about the history of places and their daily norms! I loved that our driver answered all of our questions and gave us so much information about themselves both from a tourist point as well as in insider point. He was so funny.

For example; they make limestone for toothpaste and their children go to half days of school split into day and evening classes so they can help their families work. They are required uniforms. They waste nothing since their extras must be imported and not everyone can afford those things. Their roads are only wide enough for one car and the driving is crazy. I would have wrecked in no time had it not been for our skilled driver! Their main money making is the tourists themselves. I know it sounds silly but it's weird to see American things such as a KFC in places like this. It kind of took away a little of the authenticity of the culture. I love the different kinds of flowers and the ocean colors!!!! I recommend anyone to visit this beautiful island!!!

PRISON

I don't agree with prison. They get to not work and watch TV and read all day. Nap when they want to and take more naps. They are all in great shape. They get free meals, fresh outfits, plenty of free time, and medical care. And we pay for it all with our taxes. I think they should suffer for their consequences with harder punishment. No television and hard work. Perhaps our system is not teaching them anything or they would not keep returning. Why should criminals live better than those who work every day and yet still can't afford hot water, clean clothing, or maybe even a bed to sleep in? Our justice system needs to be harsher. On average it takes 48,000 dollars to house one inmate for one year. That more than the average low income American. Granted I don’t quite agree with "an eye for an eye" but I do agree in actual punishment. Granted there are some criminals who cannot be rehabilitated such as child molesters and murders and should face the severest of punishment, but there are also those who crowd the jails who are petty thieves and drug takers. Teach them a good lesson and let them know there are no second chances. Punishment should fit the crime and we should not have to pay for their crimes with our hard-earned money. Granted it is probably hard with different cultures living in one place all trying to be "top dog" and killing each other to survive; rape and stabbing within the walls; but that also shows there isn't enough control within the walls either. I vote the hard-violent offenders get everything but what it takes to survive taken away. No perks. The thieves need harsh punishment to make them think next time. Repeaters need no mercy.

AREA 51

A mystery. A naval base? A UFO holding pen? Such a controversial secret. Their security is obvious with signs on fence posts around the arid base that say they will shoot on sight and being blacked out on Google maps. It is human nature to be curious of what is hidden. I think it is just another government base used to store and test new weapons. Is there a UFO there? No, but I do think that there is life beyond us. How can we be alone in such an endless universe? How can we be only type of creatures to exist with such miracles in nature just on earth? I believe there is proof in ancient times that something of the paranormal may have visited. (I watch a lot of "Ancient Aliens"). Of course, this could have been gods or angels or some higher beings teaching our feeble beings how to survive in such a harsh world. I don't believe we have been abducted or experimented on. If there is a race far advanced enough to fly to our planet in ancient time then why would they need to study us now? I think they would have already harvested their own little group of us on their own home planet. If there were a race advanced enough to come to our planet then why aren’t they here now? Why aren’t they helping us learn how not to destroy ourselves or to solve our own mysteries? Yes, there must be something more than just us, but I don’t think they have any knowledge of us. I think they are just like us trying to discover their own planet as well as beyond. Will we ever really find each other before one species or the other is destroyed by their own ways? Most likely not. This is just another one of man's mysteries and theories to a possibility of us being the only miracles alive in a seeming endless universe. I don't believe we have hidden proof here in Area 51. I think it's just a military base.

CRAZY CREATIVITY

Studies show that one third of all famous writers and artists all suffer from some sort of mental illness. That's six times more than that of the general population.

Among those famous are Virginia Woolf, Earnest Hemingway, Edgar Allen Poe, Emily Dickenson, and F. Scott Fitzgerald. Perhaps those who we think are the most disillusioned actually see the small truths in the world and its cruelty and injustice is just too much to bear. Perhaps these minds who were thought to have been ill were the ones most in touch with themselves and the world around them. They were able to not only see what others were blind to but felt the passion to try to tell others of what was really there. They went crazy not from what they saw but because no one understood or heard them. Take a look at how some of the ill minded grew from. Most of them started out from poverty and abuse and strove to overcome and succeed despite others thinking that they couldn't. Here they are now centuries past still being thought of as geniuses. Some overcame and thrived while some battled themselves and lost to their own devices yet in some manner was still able to leave an inspirational mark on generations to come. A mark they strove for and never achieved until after death. A mark they never knew would happen. Perhaps if they knew their work would have become success and they would be remembered forever some of their fates would not have been so tragic and their lives not so full of suffering. They say the biggest battle you fight is the one you fight with yourself. Perhaps one's own demise is what you discover from within. Hmmmm....... Creativity from suffering?

SIGHT REGAINED

Are there drawbacks to regaining sight to a completely blind person? Yes possibly. In England a man was restored his sight at the age of 52 from a surgical procedure but has become so accustomed to his darkness he began to experience issues. Depth perception was very difficult for he was used to feeling and not seeing. He also had trouble relating to common objects. What he saw blindly was not what he saw with sight. Eventually; he could not handle his new ability and shut himself away in his purposely darkened apartment so he could live as he had used to. Guess not all would consider it a miracle to gain what they had never had. Some wishes are not always what they seem once granted.

LILLITH: THE LEGENDARY TALE

A female demon of the night who supposedly flies around searching for newborn children either to kidnap or strangle them. Also, she sleeps with men to seduce them into creating demon sons. Legends told about Lilith are ancient. The myths of Lilith being Adam's first wife seem to relate to the Babylonian Goddess Belili. To the Canaanites, Lilith was Baalat, the "Divine Lady." On a tablet she was addressed as Lillake. One story is that God created Adam and Lilith as twins joined together at the back. She demanded equality with Adam, failing to achieve it, she left him in anger. This is sometimes accompanied by a Muslim legend that after leaving Adam Lilith slept with Satan. In another version of the myth of Lilith, she was Adam's first wife before Eve. Adam married her because he became tired of coupling with animals, a common Middle-Eastern herdsmen practice, though the Old Testament declared it a sin. Adam tried to make Lilith lie beneath him and she would not meet this demand of male dominance. She cursed Adam and moved to a new home by the Red Sea. Adam complained to God who then sent three angels to bring Lilith back to Eden. Lilith refused the angels and cursed them. While by the Red Sea Lilith became a lover to demons and producing 100 babies a day. The angels said that God would take these demon children away from her unless she returned to Adam. When she did not return, she was punished accordingly and then God gave Adam Eve. Even though the story of Lilith disappeared from the Bible, her daughters haunted men for over a thousand years. It was well into that Middle Ages that Jews still manufactured amulets to keep away the demon daughters. Supposedly they were lusty she-demons who copulated with men in all their dreams. Christians adopted the belief of the demon daughters calling them harlots of hell. Monks attempted to fend them off by sleeping with their hands over their genitals, clutching a crucifix. Even though most of the Lilith legend is derived from Jewish folklore, descriptions of the Lilith demon appear in Iranian, Babylonian, Mexican, Greek, Arab, English, German, Oriental and Native American legends. Also, she sometimes has been associated with legendary and mythological characters such as the Queen of Sheba and Helen of Troy. In medieval Europe she was proclaimed to be the wife, concubine, or grandmother of Satan. Men who experienced sexual dreams believed they had been seduced by Lilith. It was thought each time a Christian had a wet dream, Lilith laughed. According to legend Lilith's attraction for children comes from the belief that God took her demon children from her when she did not return to Adam. It was believed that she launched a reign of terror against women in childbirth and newborn infants, especially boys. However, it also was believed that the three angels who were sent to bring her back to Adam forced her to swear that whenever she saw their names or images on amulets that she would leave the infants and mothers alone. As late as the 18th century, it was a common practice in many cultures to protect new mothers and their infants with amulets against Lilith. Males were most vulnerable during the first week of life, girls during the first three weeks. Frequently amulets were place in the four corners and throughout the room. If a child laughed while sleeping then it was taken as a sign that Lilith was present. Tapping the child on the nose made her go away.

CRYOGENICS

The first person to be cryogenically frozen was a 73-year-old psychologist, Dr. James Bedford, who was suspended in 1967. For the whole body to be frozen it's a 250,000 annual cost and 50,000 annually for just your head. You legally have to be proven clinically dead. I'm not so sure I would choose this option no matter how rich I happened to be. For one; no one has been unfrozen and no one even knows for sure if you can successfully be reanimated. Another reason is how you will turn our after "reanimation". There could be physical damage to cells, tissue damage, and even brain damage. Would you have a memory? Would you have to relearn to do simple tasks? Would it be like the patients who have been in a coma for a long time to have to have rehab and strengthen and relearn everything again? Consider this: Most participants have died from disease or old age. What's to say there will be a cure from whatever may have taken your life when your "contract" ends and you are due to return? At an older age will you be able to explore and discover what the future holds and handle all of its new advances? Did these people expect things to remain unchanged when they returned? Will we be able to handle what the future holds? Look at how fast technology changes. Almost every day tasks would become challenges for these people. Where would you live and work? How would you get from one place to another? Will you have an assistant to reinstate you into the newer world? All of your family would be gone. Would you track down your descendants? How would they react? Mentally and emotionally could we cope? The first one to be reanimated would be a complete lab rat anyway. Who would want to live as a science experiment? More controversial; would you have a soul? Does it stay with you or come back if you have been frozen 400 years? What went through the minds of these participants who said yes to this? If it were me to awake in the future I would want a full functioning young body and a program to help me fit back into civilization. Although still psychologically I don't know I could handle knowing I was alone or even adjust to what the new world would consist of both culturally and technologically. Even the smallest things would be different. Speech, dialect, slang, dress, technology, and even manners. Some cryo-biologists predict that the first cryonic revival might occur somewhere around the year 2040. Is that when the first "contract" runs out? I am hoping that before they try this on a human they have done plenty of research on animals or maybe even a few convicts (they deserve to be lab rats anyway). The most morbid to me…. Placing my head on another's body… who is to say the body won't reject the head or that everything will work like it is supposed to. That would be a complex process in itself. Could a previously frozen body endure such a technical surgery and how would they know the medical history of that body? What if they hated that body; can they trade for a new one? So many possibilities and too many questions for such an advanced possibility.

BULLY

I don't understand kids today. They are constantly picking at and on each other. As parent are we not teaching our kids how to deal with conflicts and how their actions hurt others? Are we missing showing them how respect works? I am saddened by these children who commit suicide because of bullies. It seems as though no matter what positive things we say to our children and how much we encourage them they are still stuck on what their friends say. I try so hard to instill that they should be themselves and blow off what others think. I try to teach them to treat others as they would want to be treated. I try to teach them to turn the other check and be the better person in drama. I encourage them love who they are no matter what other people may say or think. I never know for sure of my words matter or get through to my teens, but I pray that it does. Schools allow bullying too much and parents need to take a stand. Even worse is that there are parents who encourage and often bully right along with their children. Are they trying to be their friend or a parent? How can you encourage anger and hatred in a world that needs more peace and love? Everyone has experienced the bully. Some of us has even been the bully and regretted what we've done. We all know, even as adults, we still remember these people who did us wrong. Do you want to be remembered as that person? Do you want your child remembered as that person? Let's stop the bullying!!!

THANKFUL

- I am thankful for my wonderful step- daughters who make me proud daily.
- My sweet and wonderful husband who loves me just as I am.
- My college education.
- My job even though I tend to complain about it sometimes.
- A great running vehicle.
- The Internet!!!!!
- My favorite puppies who always cuddle when I'm sad.
- My family who is always there telling me they care!!!
- Getting published!!!!!!
- My warm beautiful home

- My wonderful and supportive friends
- Creativity
- Being and aunt and sister and daughter.
- My grandma!!!
- A warm bed to sleep in
- Books! Books! Books!
- Chocolate!
- High heels and dresses!!
- Night and day!
- My own security.
- Being proud of myself.
- Inside happiness
- My career.
- Nature's beauty; when I stop and see it.
- Getting to travel the world with my sisters Bec and Cyndi!
- New family beginnings.
- Food on the dinner table!!
- My stepchildren allowing me to watch them grow into beautiful young ladies!

- My children's successes.

LOTTERY WINNER

What would you do if you won the lottery? Everyone says they will pay off their debts and buy a new home or car and use whatever is left to help family or a charity. I would say I would do the same thing. There have been stories of those who win and splurge themselves back to broke. They say that the money made them crazy and they wish they had never won it. They walked away in worse shape than when they began because of greed and impulses. Money made them change cars, houses, ways if living, and even spouses. So how do the already rich not react the same way? Is their accountant in charge and they get an allowance? Are they more careful than the impulsive winners because they earned it? What would you do with your winnings? I would become settled and debt free. I would invest a large sum for the future and help my family. I would donate to a charity. I would ensure my retirement of non-stop traveling. Here are a few people who did not benefit from their winnings: William Post: $16.2 million in Pennsylvania Lottery. In 1988, William "Bud" Post won a $16.2 million jackpot in the Pennsylvania state lottery. That was the start of his problems. An ex-girlfriend sued him for a share of winnings and won, his brother hired a hit man to try to kill him hoping to inherit some winnings, and other relatives bugged him constantly for money. Within one year, Post was $1 million in debt and filed for bankruptcy. He now lives on food stamps and a $45 a month stipend. Evelyn Adams: $5.4 million in New Jersey Lottery. In the mid-'80s, Adams won the lottery twice; once in 1985 and again in 1986 to defy all odds against her. The New Jersey native won a cool $5.4 million but was a heavy gambler. And with Atlantic City being located in New Jersey, it wasn't long before Adams had lost all her money. Today, she now lives in a trailer park and is flat broke. Billy Bob Harrell Jr.: $31 million in Texas

Lottery. A Pentecostal preacher working as a stock boy at Home Depot hit the $31 million jackpot back in 1997. At first, life was good with Billy Bob buying a ranch, six other homes, and some new cars. Like many others who win the lottery, he was unable to simply say no when people asked him for a handout. Later in life he divorced his wife and eventually committed suicide, the stress apparently too much to handle for this lottery winner.

MY COMMANDMENTS

- Thou shall not rape
- Thou shall not kill
- Thou shall not steal
- Thou shall not own another person
- Thou shall not beat a spouse or child
- Thou shall not control another physically, mentally, financially, or emotionally.
- Thou shall not limit another's freedoms
- Thou shall support the bed they made.
- Thou shall worship free of danger and judgment.
- Thou shall live in a manner that supports love and morals.

MIND READER

Imagine if you could read minds! Would you want to? Would you let others read your mind? I don't think I would want such a power. I would not want to know what people really think (
mainly about me). I wouldn't want to hear what sickos have to say. I would not want to know how sick the “normal” people I know might be. I don’t want to know their secrets and their
fetishes. Although if you knew if there was danger coming or a person who was a sicko could you stop them? Would you or should you change fate? Would you have the bravery and strength to come forward and save another's life? Would you try to become a hero and continuously put your life at risk for

others? Would this act in itself become old or mentally tasking? You know you would be judged for your special power. Even criticized and called a freak. Maybe even feared. Perhaps even captured and tested on like a lab rat by government scientists. A secret like this would have to remain so for there would be others who would want to copy your power or use you for their will.

COUNTERFIET AIRBAGS

There has been a warning in the news about if you take your car to be repaired after a wreck that your airbag could be replaced with a counterfeit. They stated to make sure you order your new airbag from the dealer yourself. That lately repair shops have been placing fakes to save money. How can you truly and knowingly place a fake airbag knowing you may risk the life of the person driving that car? How can you move forward knowing that you are betraying the trust of your customer? Where are the morals here!

THE CASE OF BILLY B BY CINDY VINE

This book is wonderfully written and very heartbreaking. Its view on child abuse is blunt and has the view of both adult and child which you don't normally see in books of such topic. I love the writer's style and that she used both the parents view and the child's views of event happenings without confusing the readers with big jumps or time jumps. This book touched my heart and proved that sometimes you have to let go even if it's the hardest thing you can do. I highly recommend this book and I know it's available on kindle but unsure about paperback.

LOOK OF DEATH

I find this interesting. That when a person is passing there is a moment in which you can feel all things change. Even their appearance is instantaneous. It's as if you can tell the moment the soul escapes the body. The body goes ashen and loses one degree per hour according to criminal researchers. The temperature is how detectives know how long someone has passed. I remember when I was young I got ahold of the video series "Faces of Death" and there is a clip in particular on one of the videos that had always stuck with me. This magician was performing a timed trick to where he had to escape before the anvil crushed his head. He was unsuccessful and it fell. I cannot forget the instant look of his body after his death. He automatically stiffened and lost all color. It's like you could see the exact moment his spirit left his body. It was not a gruesome scene in a sense. You didn't see the skull crush or blood splatter or drain. It was a clean and instant death. Call me sick but I rewound that video on that one spot. The change and look of death was intriguing to me. It was intriguing because it was instant. Like I said before; it was almost like seeing the soul leave. A scientist once measured the weight of the body upon death and found a 21-gram difference. Does our soul weigh 21 grams? Did his soul rise up and see his situation? I don't remember if there was a live crowd during that magic show although I can guess there was. I can't imagine how all of those people reacted and dealt with such a scene. Just seeing the event on TV was enough for me to remember it from childhood let alone seeing something like that right before my face. Even though I was young when I saw this video I can still picture it perfectly in my mind. You could say I'm perhaps traumatized.

BEING RELATED TO EMILY DICKENSON

I feel an odd connection with this woman. Though of course we have never met it seems as though we may know each other. There are so many coincidences that make it seem so. Her father Edward was born January 1st. I have an aunt born the same day. Her birthday is in December making her a Capricorn the same as I. Although she has brothers and sisters she felt as an only child. I am an only child. She preferred solitude and has a passion of writing the same as I. Hear idealism of nature, values, and religion relate to me as well. It's amazing how much I resemble this woman. Except for the fact that I am not bound to my home.... For now. There is a book called "The Life of Emily Dickenson" which is very captivating and detailed. (Available on kindle)

AMNESIA

To suffer from amnesia would be such a tragedy. To spin one's life out of control. There a many types. Retrograde is before a certain time like an accident or trauma. This can often be regained in time. Family members can show pictures and tell stories to help promote the return of some memories. Ante grade is where you can't remember any new information. I would have to start a diary to keep new memories in so that I could go back and try to reflect. That would be like the movie "50 First Dates" where he makes new videos for his girlfriend and then wife to keep her updated on her life. I guess in this aspect you would always be forced to live in the moment. I would have to be very descriptive though. Dissociative Fugue is where the person has no hope of regaining any memories of who they are or their past so often they travel elsewhere and begin again to find a new identity. I could not imagine starting all over from scratch and possible never knowing where I came

from or who I may have been. I would always wonder if the life I left was one that I wanted or if it was a good thing that things had changed. I would
always wonder who and what I had left behind and probably research my past self if I had any
information. In this type of case it would probably be best to not have any leads and just start fresh otherwise always needing closure. I would travel continuously if I knew I had nothing to return to. Of course, there are those of us now who wish we could just drop everything and run away to start over anyway. Some do……

I KNEW HE WAS GONE

Do you get the feeling when you know someone you love has passed? This feeling has touched me twice. That moment when you feel like something has happened but you don't know what yet. That strange gut/ brain rush. Perhaps they told you and you didn't know until later. The first time I felt this was when my grandfather passed. I woke in the middle of the night in a sweat and had a strange feeling something was wrong. I knew he was sick but I passed it off as worry and went back to sleep. The next day I went to work and asked the boss the policy on bereavement just in case. Within a half hour of finding out work procedure my grandmother arrived to tell me he had passed in the night. When I was called to the office before I even saw her or knew she was there I knew what had happened. My throat already began to swell like I needed to cry. Then I saw her. She didn't even have to speak. The second time was a dear friend. He was ill and we went to visit him. We knew his time was limited but didn't know how long. We each took turns visiting and saying what we needed to. We left after a while and on the ride home I got that feeling again. My throat swelling like I should cry and my brain in a rush. Then my phone rang. They told us he had passed shortly after we left. Do we all just have a special connection to some? Such a deep connection that even when we are not around we still feel another's emotions. Maybe we somehow can connect unknowingly to another's mind or soul? All I know is that something was there… something telling me what was so before I should have known…. something higher or deeper than I could ever explain….

Section Two: Poetry

BURDEN

I carry a burden upon my soul;
Like buckets of water upon a monk's shoulders.
I carry stress within my mind;
Like pockets of rocks; just weighted down.
I carry doubt of everything;
Filling my heart with silent grief.
Like a whipped dog that lies down upon each comforting reach
Some days are easy to ignore it all
Pretend I don't care and put up my wall
Some days are hard to just walk down the hall
I drag my feet and the tears just fall
Some days I am everything and some days I'm nothing
Some days I'm proud and some days

I’m not Deep inside
Torn in two
My own disease we can’t find a cure
No one will understand why one day I laugh and one day I cry
Here’s another pill to mask the pain
And here’s another to force you happy.

COMA

Between a dream and reality
I cannot move or speak
I cannot see
I feel your touch upon my hand
I hear your voice echo in the room
A voice full of sadness
Full of fear
Inside I squirm and scream
My brain races as I fail to make limbs do as commanded
I am here
I am well The machine is wrong

I hear you and I feel you
I'm still inside this frozen body
Don't give up hope on me yet.

FALL

Once upon a fresh fall day
Golden rays light the field of hay
A railed off bridge
Hovering over gleaming waters
An isle of trees on either side
Rustling leaves under the gentle breeze
Crisp colors dazzle the eyes
Colors that fall with each breeze to pass
Falling down around me and into the stream
Reds, yellows, and fiery oranges fall like rain
Breezes scoot them across the ground
Flipping and flying like a spirit with no

care
Carrying them here and there
Fate deciding where they shall lay.

PURPOSE

Ocean waves crash the cliffs
Shaping and carving the rock beneath its wrath
Slowly with time they shift their appearance
Pieces breaking off and changing their purpose.
Like a person whose opinions change
After waves of experience and pains.
The soul and heart whose pieces break.
Whose life's purpose changes with the winds.

MATERIALS

Material
Why does this THING bring me joy?
A temporary joy
Am I filling a void with a new object?
The joy won't last.
The search for such an item to bring a rush of happiness
A day to two and I'm said again
This thing does not bring me joy
This thing does not fill the void
Material
Why am I searching for things when I should search inside?
Why am I excited by a quick buy?
Why

MOVING FORWARD

I look upon the past
Unwillingly
It flashes across my mind

Unexpectedly
How can I move forward when you haunt my mind?
I cannot escape these thoughts
I cannot escape my memories
I cannot suppress the past
I want to forget
I want to move forward
I have forgiven and tried again
But the thoughts remain
The heart still broken
The soul still soured I want to move forward
But you have held me back
Go away pain
Go away thoughts

DEAR CHILD

Dear child always on my mind
Dear sweet sweet child of mine
Don't take that path of darkness
Don't take the road with no light

What seems like fun will have no end in sight
Look around and see the consequence
See the tracks the devil has laid
Smart child
Wise child beyond your years
Don't be blind and let the devil have your souls
Because even if you manage to get it back
Beaten and damaged you will remain
A part inside no one can console

LOVE

My love for undying
Unwavering
Unchanging
My love for you the deepest
Year after year
We close the gap
My lover
My friend

My shoulder
My confidant
My love for you as constant as the moon rises nightly
Years make us grow fonder
Togetherness wiser
Passion deeper
I can only wish for more years to come
To equal the years of happiness we have had
I can only hope our love lasts forever
And nothing ever gets in our way
For our hearts have become one
A soul mate found If failure were to come I would never be whole again

DOOR

One door opened and another closed
Life's path changed again
Unexpectedly I'm led down another road

Life’s a journey
Ever-changing
Circumstances and situations come
to test my strength
But nothing will knock me down
Success and happiness is what I grow
on
What I focus on
When one door closes another opens
Leading me to where I belong
Where fate and purpose needs me
Success will drive me
Failure will only teach me
I will walk through each new door
I will stride through confident and
strong

IT WILL COME

My end will arrive
Unknowingly when
I am sure to leave a mark
Be it big or small
Be it on one person or many

This I will never know for sure
To make a change on this world
Or to inspire the soul of just one more
Labor and leisure past my time quickly
Remorse is cureless; to be dealt with tact.
Resentment must pass; forgiven like anger.
Pain to be numbed with positivity
It will come
My end here on earth
Bury me with no box covered in flowers
Let me return to earth
Let my soul decide its path
Don't cry on behalf.
Be happy you knew me.
Be proud you placed a smile upon my face. Be satisfied you will remain in my memory even when I'm past
It will come.

BOOK

***Inside the crisp pages
In another's thoughts
Creativity from a dream?
Substance from events
I lose myself in their words.
I become one of their characters.
I play the scenes in my head as
though I may have been there.
Feeling and description take my mind.
Take me away from one's own realm.
A dream when awake.
Reading each sentence as if I had
said it myself.
Reading each paragraph twice as to
collect all detail.
The story that stays long after the
pages are finished
The story that holds the heart when
the book is laid upon its shelf.
Those are the ones memories and
lessons arrive.
Thank god for those writers with
passion. Thank them for their never-
ending hard work.***

Their detail for words and passion for thought.
Their endless nights of preparing perfection.

HERE SHE COMES

Arriving with no surprise
Right on time
Bringing chirps of birds and budding flowers with her
Rain and sun
Cloud and blue sky
Mother Nature changed her cycle
From frosty days to sun and shine
From death and damper
To growth and renewal
Warmth slowly comes
Rebirth of all things
Gracefully
Here she comes

THIS RING

This ring I wear
This symbol upon thy finger
A heart captured
A vow kept
A contract of life
Through tough and tumble
Though joy and rejoice
We grow together like entwine vine
I gave myself to him despite health and wealth
As our bodies fade with age our love will only grow.

BALANCE

In between relaxation and responsibility
In between chore and quality
In between love and work
Today's demands creates such choices
Where one soars another falls

Each path a little different
Each path leading to the same destination

DEATH

Where there is death there is also life
Where there is good there is also evil
Where there is darkness there is light
Balance among all things
Where one is bountiful one is empty
Where one is healthy another suffers sickness
Where one finds happiness another only finds pain
Balance
All leading to the same destination
Where one has decades some only have years

ONLY FOR SOME

Only for some do we really suffer.
While I fill my stomach others just a morsel
While I can heal what ails me others must suffer
While I dance in dresses others barely have a wrap
While I prance in fancy shoe others go without
My bed warm and soft while others sleep under the stars on pillows of rocks
How lucky I am and how I take advantage of this While lights and heat are of not second though
For some it's their only wish
Our riches vary in the deepest manner.
Those without hold appreciation
While those with hold a spoiled set
Those who lack appreciate love and family
Those who have honor only their

materials.

CASTLE

Walls of stone with history within
Chambers and secret doorways
Windows that always remains open
Sprits that roam the halls
Great rooms of antique valiant design
Rooms of great things of royalty and riches
Stone walkways cannot be quietly passed.
What was once the throne of a great royal?
Now remains empty except for dust and cobwebs SICKNESS
She lay in her bed wondering her time
Absorbed by cancer
Fighting for her life
She will choose when she is ready
She will think of all the wishes she had.
She will weigh her regrets.
She will think of her

accomplishments.
She will think of fear and peace.
She will worry for her family.
Will she know when to say goodbye
Will she know what to say?

BARE

I have bared my soul
Opened myself to judgment
My words flow on paper
Some written without fear.
Some written worried about others thoughts
Words flowing of pain like tears from my fingertips Joys and sorrows all on crisp paper with deep pressed inks
Chaos typed as fast as the mind can think
I've bared it all through my words
My soul shining through the letters
Word by word
Piece by piece
My soul shared with you

Bare

BUSTLE IN THE HOUSE

Work has ended for the day.
Arriving home and work begins again
Chores to sustain the home
Chasing and teaching children within
Some days flow smooth
Some day's chaos
Some days bring joy of family
Some days bring turmoil of each
owns personality
But this bustle in this house will not
last forever
One day they will be grown And all
will be much too quiet
I'll have time for me
But there only so much to occupy me
This bustle in this house
I'll enjoy while I have
The good with the bad

It's all worthwhile

AFRAID

What am I afraid of?
Not death for it is inevitable
Not success because it is of my own
Not change for that is life
Not my past for it is done
My future perhaps
Of things I cannot control
My feelings
Of thoughts that never cease
Not of others judgments For I do not lend a care
Of myself and where I may end up?
Of my failures I could have avoided?
Of my mistakes I can't take back?
What holds me in this limbo?
Why can't I set my own soul free?
Why can't I ease my own minds wondering?

LOSING MY MIND

I think I'm losing my mind.
I plaster a smile upon this face
Turmoil inside that I've lost control of
I find myself in such a daze
Never in the now
Mind wandering to past and future
In the loneliness of this home
I hear my name called
I hear whispers
Am I hearing a past soul?
Is my mind playing a trick? I see you speaking but I don't hear your words.
The lights flicker and I doubt that they really did
Paranoid and nowhere to turn
No one to ask if any of this is normal.
Dreams that never make sense
Dreams that wake me in the midst of

the night
Jerked to reality in an un-calmed state
Sleep avoids me until it's unwanted.

REFUGEE

Hiding within thyself
Lying to the soul
Mind blocking all that is traumatic
As to walk another day
Secrets not revealed
Scars not shown
Pain not spoken of
Put down and kicked around
Running from the past
Paranoid forever
The mind never letting go
Never forgetting
Never suppressing

LIPS

Lips of yours
Lips of mine
Meeting with passion
As new lovers do
We are not new lovers
Time has kept us close
Time has kept us strong
Passions for you unwavering all in all
Lips of your that speak of your love for me
Lips of yours that prove your words
Thirsty for your love no matter how much you give. YOU
Oh what you do to me!!!!
My face burns red
My blood boils
Angry thoughts racing in my mind
Oh what you do to me!!!
Everyday it's you!!
Standing in my way
Causing me hell
You say you don't mean to
You say you can't help it
You cry
Your tears used to touch me and

make me forgive you
Not anymore
Cry cry cry
Because I don't care
Your choices affect others
Your choices affect me
They rule over me like a demon spirit.

UNTITLED

If I can stop one heart from breaking
I shall not live in vain
If I can ease on life the aching
Or cool one pain,
Or help one fainting robin
Unto his nest gain ,
I shall not live in vain.
"Emily Dickenson"

UNTITLED

The soul selects her own society
Then shuts the door:
On her divine majority
Obtrude no more.
Unmoved she notes the chariots pausing
At her low gate;
Unmoved, an emperor is kneeling
Upon her mat
I've known her from an ample nation
Choose one; Then close the valves of her attention
Like stone.
"Emily Dickenson"

LIFE

A life changed
A life hindered
He doesn't listen;

and she does what she wants
One person who holds a heart in their
hand gets it knocked into the sand
She picks it up and holds it out again
Only to have it dropped once more
This heart can only handle so much
Before its pieces can't be picked up
again So now I wonder as I pick them
up are the last slivers worth dropping
for you again?

Section Three: Inspirational Quotes

"Silence contributes as much to the sound of a poem as the words do." - Emily Dickenson

"I was writing poetry always. While I swept the steps, washed the dishes, completed the laundry. I carried a pencil and scraps of paper in my apron to ensure that my best thoughts would be captured as they occurred."-Emily Dickenson

"I feared that my preoccupation with poetry annoyed my family for I was hearing only a fraction of what they said to me. I was more interested in the sound inside my head; insistent words that would later become my poem."- Emily Dickenson

"Words, set in type, can live forever. Immortality."- Emily Dickenson

"But to see the real person you must consult the page; read the work."- Emily Dickenson

"Silence contributes as much to the sound of a poem as words do."- Emily Dickenson

"I like to write the special words, giving them the weight of ink they deserve. But it's the linking of one to another, building the blinding thought, which ignites my Soul. I didn't know at first that it was poetry I was making."- Emily Dickenson.

"I'd given then most private thing I could: my poetry. Seeing my work is like peeling back my skin. I was more than naked; I was raw."- Emily Dickenson

"Give more than you take."-Anonymous

“Even the best turn cruel in crisis.”- Anonymous

“All I have to give: I gave”- Anonymous

“Perhaps we aren’t meant to be all knowing and not all mysteries are meant to be solved. How boring life would be if we knew all the answers.” - Dan Barker

"If spirituality were wiped out it would be created differently. If scientific knowledge were wiped out it would be rediscovered with a matching result.”-Unknown

“Do not Inflict pain as which you would not want yourself. Before an action switch your shoes and views.”-Anonymous

“A lie is a lie even if everyone believes it.

The truth is the truth even if no one believes it."- Anonymous

"Bury me bare so I may return to earth. So flora and fauna may dine upon me as I did them."-Anonymous

"Everyone you me et has certain features that grab your attention and you fall in love with."- Anonymous

"It's okay if you don't have a cheerleader; still chase that dream. The only approval you need is your own."- Unknown

About The Author

Jennifer Johnson is from a small town in Indiana. She is a scuba diver, traveler, small time actress, step-mother of two, and career woman. Jennifer began writing at an early age and the passion has stuck with her since producing several single and collaborative publications. She has been locally nominated in the "Who's Who" of literary arts, is a member of the local Writer's Guild, and has been nominated in Indiana Emerging Authors. Jennifer's publications can be found on createspace.com, amazon.com, and her local bookstores.

Reviews

Steven A Williams-Author, Poet

These pieces are written with such vulnerability, honesty, and intimacy, they can't help but to be deeply touching, and create quite a personal introspective look into the writer's life. They are stitched together to tell a sad, inspiring, and hopeful story of love, family, challenge, strength, and triumph. They are also displayed in an original format serving the double purpose of being a child's advice to carry them through all the changes of life which is culminated in "My Child", one of the best pieces in the collection. This writer has an incredibly strong voice throughout her work which is one of the most important building blocks of a great poet!

Steven A Williams-Author, Poet
Random Thoughts

Here is another great collection of poetry and thought by a wonderful independent author. This one far more vulnerable and personal than the last which makes it a pleasure and an introspective journey to read. The first section contains some great philosophy and conversation starting thought reflection, but the second section steals the show! Beautiful, fluid, and in most cases, brilliant poetry showing an amazing level of maturity and evolution from the authors previous work. This book is a wonderful collection and a benefit to any mind and soul to read!

Kimberly DuBois
Random Thoughts

This collection is very moving. It is introspective, thoughtful and deeply felt. The author poses deep questions and writes with emotion. She is being genuine and honest in this book, which I enjoyed. A book that makes you think!

If you enjoyed this; try this:

- ✓ Random Thoughts
- ✓ One Mind's Words I & II
- ✓ Our Journey
- ✓ Red Eyes
- ✓ In Too Deep

Made in the USA
Monee, IL
21 October 2026

66035054R00062